Jerly,
Grow from within!
Lon Chesnutt

A Devotional for Progressive Christians

LON B. CHESNUTT

LifeRich Publishing is a registered trademark of The Reader's Digest Association, Inc.

LifeRich Publishing books may be ordered through booksellers or by contacting:

LifeRich Publishing
1663 Liberty Drive
Bloomington, IN 47403
www.liferichpublishing.com
1 (888) 238-8637

ISBN: 978-1-4897-0984-4 (sc)
ISBN: 978-1-4897-0983-7 (e)

Library of Congress Control Number: 2016916341

Print information available on the last page.

LifeRich Publishing rev. date: 12/21/2016

Preface

As language is important for our understandings, the use of very ancient words and phrases has become problematic for many Christians. This brief writing tries to give an alternative way for understanding scripture and articulating implications in these tumultuous days.

These particular Biblical passages follow a guide found in Reuben Job's PRAYING IN A NOISEY WORLD and then utilize the list of "Suggested Scripture Lessons" in the 1992 edition of THE UNITED METHODIST BOOK OF WORSHIP. Out of the scripture passage for the day, I have selected what seems to me the key verse for comments. The pattern of selection is not as significant as is the method of treatment for each scripture passage, which is explained below. Bible quotations are from the New Revised Standard Version.

Introduction

This booklet was first prepared as a 'Prayer Journal' of my own reflections. After some rereading and thinking, it seemed that it might be helpful for others who are having difficulty with an older form of personal devotions. Thus in following the traditional pattern of scripture reading, reflection, and a brief prayer, I have tried to explore the relationship of Bible reading and it's meaning for one's personal life.

The use of non-traditional language in addressing God or thinking about Deity is an attempt to move away from the understanding of Divinity as an outside source of power. Traditionally, this super-power breaks into our lives with revelations about what we should believe. Instead, these pages are designed to help us shift the source of responsibility. The Divine is already in the workings of our own thinking, feeling, and decision-making inner self. Our task is to acknowledge that presence and then take responsibility for what we do.

Day 1

Ephesians 2: 8 – 10 *"Grace has saved you.... For we are what he has made us...."*

The relationship between initiative of the Deity and initiative of the individual has always been a concern for me. Earlier in my life and thinking it seemed that scripture and Christian teaching proclaimed that God acted first and planted whatever good things I did within me, as the above passage can read.

But it's only come to me in recent times that there's an alternative understanding of the way God can work—not 'Deus ex Machina'—God coming from an outside place into my life—but God being a part of my life and using who I already am to face every issue coming before me. Then I can make the most responsible judgment or decision possible. This shifts the understanding of Deity from an external force or power into an inside creativity that is always there, ready to be utilized. It's more than me, but I must 'take the initiative' for any decisions made. Perhaps that's the way that we take action on behalf of the Deity.

Prayer: "Holder of who I am, bring together new strands of possibility that are within me and direct them toward the character of love, which I would like to become. For the sake of a fuller life, it's time."

Day 2

John 8: 31- 38 *"You will know the truth, and the truth will make you free."*

It's important to remember your history and to draw ideas from it, but it's also important to realize that you should not be bound by whatever happened back then. Staying with only what you can remember and claim from the past is dangerous because that closes your eyes and ears to what is happening around you. It especially blocks out what may just be opening up beyond you.

My task is to find ways to test an idea thoroughly enough for its values before making a major investment of my time and energy.

For me, the struggle is to decide which new door to open and explore. There are so many opportunities and so many limits to time and energy.

Prayer: "Spirit of Wonderment, continue to pull together different aspects of my experiences into new conclusions and new opportunities for my life so that every day is a joy to behold. In the name of Jesus the explorer, affirmative."

Day 3

Psalm 100 *"For the Lord is good, his steadfast love endures forever, and his faithfulness to all generations."*

These are my favorite five verses in the Hebrew Bible. They summarize an understanding of the Divine in such a positive and joyful manner.

This closing verse underscores the basic faith or trust of the entire Bible; it is an affirmation of the goodness of all that exists. It includes the natural world, all the animals in all their forms, and the total human journey. This attitude would stop wars and change the world if humans could only come to adopt it.

Only the Divine maintains 'steadfast love' because that is a form of existence that we humans attain only to a partial degree, though we hold it as an ideal goal of life.

To include 'all generations' in this permanent attitude is one of the most comforting statements ever made. It counts me 'in' as valuable!

Prayer: "Truth-releaser that is deeply protected within my psyche, unleash also the freedom that honesty nurtures in the spirit so that I can be one step nearer the wholeness that is intended in our creation. Spoken in the name and power of forgiveness, as it is."

Luke 11: 1- 10 *"Your kingdom comes on earth as in heaven."*

Silent time in one's 'private time' can be difficult. It's hard to close out other thoughts as distractions. One possibility is to see them as a way the Divine, or God, or the 'More' becomes accessible within us. Then you can deal with them and explore their meaning at the moment.

Luke's version is the short form of the Lord's Prayer and it speaks directly on needs and responsibility without dressing it up with fancy adjectives or phrases.

Including regular scripture reading as part of daily routine in 'private time' is a good practice to include. It puts you in contact with the faith tradition as a starting place. The temptation is to approach scripture from a scholarly or historian's point of view asking, "What was the author trying to convey at this point?" But recently, Walter Wink's Biblical methodology as a New Testament teacher centers around asking a more basic question, "What is this passage saying to me at this moment?" The real task today is to include both these questions.

Prayer: "Spirit of Wonderment, continue to pull together different aspects of my experiences into new conclusions and new opportunities for my life. Enrich every day as a joy to behold. In the name of Jesus the explorer, affirmative."

Day 5

John 10: 1 – 7, 10 *"I came that they may have life, and have it abundantly."*

The Jesus' Seminar, in their evaluation of the Gospels, claims that Jesus probably didn't say anything like the way it's recorded in John. This leaves one with the question, 'What is the community around John trying to say about gatekeepers and the sound of the master's voice?'

I think that by the time John was written, around 100-110 CE, the split between the synagogues and Christians had occurred. It was very important to know which community was yours. Thus the Christians wanted to be sure that they were hearing and following the leadership of Jesus in what they were trying to be.

In our time, Progressive Christianity has become a means for people to understand both the faith of Jesus and choose a contemporary interpretation that makes sense in the 21st. century.

Prayer: "Thou Presence who is always listening, speak to me through the life of Jesus and his constant sense of what life was about. Teach me how to listen to my deepest urges on what to do. In the name of truth, so be it."

Day 6

Acts 1:21 – 26 *'Show us which one of these two you have chosen to the place in this ministry and apostleship....'*

This early scene in Acts was after Peter had taken leadership. They needed someone to replace Judas among the twelve apostles.

The choosing of Mathias has always raised questions for me about what happened to the other fellow, Joseph? I wondered if he continued in any type of leadership in the earliest Christian community and what that might have been. Casting lots or throwing dice has always sounded like a brutal way to choose between two qualified leaders. It is such a stark divider between winners and losers.

It's also very inconsistent with Jesus' methodology. His approach encouraged everyone, including women, to follow 'The Way' to the maximum of their ability. That could be a great theme for a novel or movie along the line of "The Loser's Victory" or "Overlooked".

Prayer: "Reality beyond words and images, focus my attention on the combinations that give me an ever new opportunity to be chosen by you for special ministry. In the spirit of new decisions every day, go for it!"

Day 7

Colossians 2: 6 – 9 *"All the fullness of God lives in Jesus."*

This sentence goes with much of the reading and thinking in Progressive Christianity. If you want to see what God is like and what he loves, go look to Jesus. For our time, looking at Jesus is looking at what humans can be in their most loving fashion. In spite of the many people trying to follow an impulse to love and help other folks, there remain the ones who have been warped by hatred and lust for power. How to replace the patterns of hatred and disrespect with an attitude of tolerance and friendship is difficult to imagine right now.

Karen Armstrong's book on violence (FIELDS OF BLOOD) may be a way toward understanding as a beginning. It proposes moving beyond self-interest to seeking the best for other people.

Compassion is within everyone's basic make-up. Armstrong concludes that responsibility for our world rests with humans, both religious and non-religious. Can we move through responsibility to freely given compassion?

Prayer: "Reality beyond thinking and feeling, unite within me a new sense of what is vital in life and show me what commitment can do with the resources I am. In the confidence that integrity is a spiritual gift, so be it."

Day 8

Romans 8:26 – 28 *"God makes all things work together for good for those who love the Lord."*

I've been thinking about what is the interior force or entity that represents the Divine if there is no entity 'out there' somewhere. It's hard to conceptualize anything within the body. All I can visualize are corpuscles or ganglia, and that's not very encouraging. I'm left with the 'Mysterious' with a capital 'M', but that's not very helpful even if I dramatize its pronunciation.

So how do all the brains, memories, thoughts, projections, hopes, and anxieties come together in what is a new thought? And in the midst of whatever is stimulating a new thought, how does one distinguish among these thoughts as to what is spiritual or God-inspired, and what is just ordinary like 'I'm hungry, I'll go to the fridge.'

It must have something to do with the kind of habits and values that one has established over a lifetime. But that answer also leads to more questions....

Prayer: "Thou Mysterious one, who keeps coming to me when I'm serious about listening for new ideas. Stimulate my brain with new ideas that challenge my habits so that life is forever being fulfilled. With trust in it all coming together, never give up."

Day 9

Psalm 25: 1 – 6 *"Lead me in your truth, and teach me, for you are the God of my salvation."*

Whether or not this was David's prayer is not important. To me, the key insight here is trying to find and follow the truth that is deep inside each one of us.

> *"If you know who you are,*
> *You'll know what to do."*

The first assumption is that there is a divine core or coming together within each person. Then there is our consciousness that can learn from it and bring those values into the working level of our brain. The rationale for doing this is the conclusion that one's 'salvation' or 'wholeness' comes when we place this divine impulse at the center of who we are.

I keep coming back to the book title of Ronald J. Greer: "If You Know Who You Are, You'll Know What to Do". That's the basis of every religion. For Christians, it's the trust factor that we experience when we proclaim Jesus as the example of the Divine. The mark of maturity is this combination of personal trust with creativity in your life.

Prayer: "Source of what is, keep on opening within me new possibilities for my resources. More fully develop my service in the world to use the thoughts that I envision. In the name of reality, yes."

Romans 8: 31 – 34 *"It is God who justifies. Who is to condemn?"*

By understanding that the Divine is within yourself, justification takes on a new perspective. It's not something that comes from an outside source or from somewhere else, but it's a shift that occurs within the self. Judgment and satisfaction can be described as gifts from someone else—the Divine. However, the experience of being justified or feeling wholeness is an entirely personal happening.

If the attitude of being justified has shifted from an external to an internal dimension, then how can anyone or anything external to the self be the source of condemnation? Someone else may have power over your job, body, movement, or even existence; but they can never control the interior psyche that makes you a self-conscious being.

> *"The experience of being justified or feeling wholeness is an entirely personal happening."*

Prayer: "Source of all life, enrich our freedom that we may take charge of who we really are and make wiser decisions about that to which we give ourselves. In the context of a completely open agenda, for sure."

Day 11

Philippians 2: 1 – 5 *"Think of yourself the way Christ Jesus thought of himself."* (THE MESSAGE, Eugene Peterson)

If Jesus was fully human, if he was just a sensitive peasant, if he hadn't encountered any great teachers, if he really was illiterate, then he becomes even more amazing and incredible! His ability to see what was going on in First century Palestine is remarkable—the societal levels in his society, the selfishness of the rich, the way society was structured against the poor, and all the injustices toward the poor.

Even more amazing was the alternative life-style he envisioned and practiced. He appealed to the hearts of people with a way to see beyond their subsistence level. He showed them a personal attitude that accepted each person just as they were and affirmed their very existence. That attitude makes him the Christ, the one who brings hope and fulfillment to everyone.

Prayer: "Always present, keep bringing to conscious memory what I already know about Jesus' life so that his attitude of openness, compassion, and curiosity become major in my life. For hope's sake, surely."

Day 12

I Corinthians 3: 10 – 17 *"Do you not know that you are God's temple and God's Spirit dwells in you?"*

Paul loved to draw people into a dialogue with himself by personally addressing them as in this question. But his purpose was always to make a point. Because his questions were rhetorical, the answer was always also in the question. Here the point is for the readers—the Christians—to realize that they have already received the Divine into their lives and that their actions should reveal that permeating presence.

> *From our example, self-care and love for those around us reveal the way to a fulfilled life.*

It's an admonition that is as true today as when Paul penned it. If you claim to be a part of a faith community, your life should show it by the manner in which you live. Paul is using the ancient respect for the temple as a metaphor for the way we present our bodies. We are the community of faith. From our example, self-care and love for those around us reveal the way to a fulfilled life.

Prayer "Thou presence that becomes like a being, surprise me with new thoughts and challenges that take me into areas untried before. In the hope of serving our larger world, be brave."

John 14: 23-26 *Those who love me will keep my word, and my Father will love them, and we will come to them and make our home with them."*

The sentence structure above make this passage sound as if the 'we will come to the lover' is an outside force joining with the already existing person and then making it a richer entity.

However, if you start with the premise that the Divine 'We--Father and Son'—are already present within the human, it shifts the understanding. Instead of an external source being added, look at what's been there all along and seek a new emphasis upon what can be created. This shift tells you to look inside yourself and use everything that's there to foster love and opportunity.

It's a new source of motivation and reliance upon who you already are. It's says, 'Go ahead, you can do whatever is needed.'

> *Go ahead, you can do whatever is needed.*

PRAYER: "Power within, open my eyes to see the possibilities that I already possess. Motivate me to be bold with creativity through the fullness already given. In the use of untested resources that are waiting, move ahead."

Isaiah 58:1-11 *Is not this the fast that I choose: to loose the bonds of injustice… to let the oppressed go free.'*

The prophet Isaiah is speaking for the Lord to the people. The message is certainly as true today as when it was first uttered. In effect, he's criticizing any ceremony or liturgy that a religious community puts together that does not deal with the injustices that are inflicted upon the people around them. He's attacking the structures of injustice that have been put in place by the powerful that give them goods and advantages at the expense of the poor and underclass.

In our time, this has more and more to do with the laws and practices that have been engineered. They give rewards to those who already have the most goods. The issue is how to change the way the system works. Can we include everyone and build justice into the foundation of the system?

> *'The issue is how to change the way the system works.'*

Prayer: "Eyes and brain that see the suffering around us. Do not stop showing the pain of others until those of us who can bring justice lead the way toward a loving society. Remembering Jesus as our model, yes."

Luke 19: 45 – 47 *"My house shall be a house of prayer."*

This sentence raises the most basic issue for a Temple, synagogue, mosque, or church—What is its purpose? Why should religious people build a religious building? What are these people supposed to do when they gather at the building? The answer that Jesus gave is that it's supposed to be a place where prayers are continually being given. As one question usually leads to another, then the real question here is: What is the meaning of prayer? We are taught early in our Christian experience that prayer is communicating with God, talking as if with a friend, listening for what God has to say to us, or asking for anything we really need.

In light of the history of thought, this shifts the issue to what kind of communication or thought is happening when you are in the act of praying? This is particularly difficult when one of the struggles occurring is the understanding of God. If the Divine is no longer understood as a separate outside creator, then asking for intervention of any type is not the purpose of prayer.

For me, this shifts the activity of prayer away from communicating with an external source and waiting for an answer. The place to begin is looking at my own internal resources and trying to understand how they can be better utilized. It places the self in the driver's seat and asks, "What are you going to do about this subject that you want to raise?" This becomes a new understanding of responsibility because the source for help is no longer someone or something outside of you. It leaves you with the task of observing what is happening, judging alternative responses, evaluating what is most important, figuring out how to respond, and then doing it. Praying seriously is hard work, but it transforms lives beginning with the one who is praying.

Prayer: "Source of my power, utilize my memory, analyzing abilities, values, and will to face squarely any opportunities that come before me today. Lead me to make the most comprehensive decisions of which I am capable. In the name of who I can be, seize the day!"

> *Serious prayer leaves you with the task of*
>
> *observing what is happening,*
> *judging alternative responses,*
> *evaluating what is most important,*
> *figuring out how to respond, and*
> *then doing it.*

Day 16

Acts 6: 2 – 7 *"It is not right that we should neglect the word of God in order to wait on tables or keep accounts."*

I'd never noticed the intent of this passage before, but it appears to me that this justifies the separation of disciples into classes. It begins as a well-intentioned motive based on a division of labor. But the unintended result of this action was to set up structures within the early Christian communities that placed authority and power with a certain group of followers.

If Luke was the author of Acts and it was written around 90 CE, then it reflects about three generations after the death of Jesus. By then the cultural prejudice of considering only men for leadership had set in. The division between the best talkers and all other tasks of a community had taken over, and a most dangerous value had established itself.

That danger, as I see it, was allowing some leaders to say, 'What we think and do is more important than what you do, therefore you are to be subordinate to our group'.

Prayer: "Gracious Spirit, who keeps loving us in spite of our bumbling attempts to love you, forgive us when we build human structures and priorities that reflect what we want rather than what is beneficial for all. Keep giving us opportunities to make corrections for the benefit of the larger good. In the sense of justice and good will, surge forward."

Matthew 9: 25 – 38 *"Then Jesus went about all the villages, teaching and proclaiming the good news of the kingdom (God's reign)…."*

The Gospel writers used a lot of hyperbole in their descriptions of what Jesus did and said. Visiting all the villages and covering 'all aspects' of the 'good news' is quite an exaggeration of what one person can actually do in a limited period of time. But this statement is right in line with what Matthew and the other authors wanted to convey about their leader— Jesus. He was a charismatic teacher, someone that you could look-up to for information and inspiration about life.

Just to be in his presence and hear him talk made a difference to the hearer. His integrity was solid, and his ideas were always given with enough wisdom and difference that you knew they were worth considering. Things came together in a way that you could experience a new understanding and be able to say, 'He's right, that's the way it is. God's rule is already right here.'

Prayer: "Motivation Source, empower me to see Jesus' humanity in ways that break through old stereotypes. Cause his directness, sensitivity, clear headedness, humor, and judgment to become models for my life. In the fullness of compassion, open my senses."

Exodus 3: 1 – 18 *"If they ask you, What is his name?..., say 'I AM has sent me to you.'"*

'What is your authority?' is the primary question in relationships at all levels—person to person, group to group, known to unknown, friend to friend, friend to enemy, nation to nation, etc. So it's basically the question of how an individual is going to relate to everyone else.

From the Judeo-Christian perspective, the source of authority has always been that God has provided me with whatever is needed. If one understands the Divine as an internal source rather than an entity out there somewhere, then authority rests with the individual. For me, I keep coming back to integrity and the total combination of all my resources that make up my being. It's the sum of who you are; that's what you have to present, to offer, and to negotiate on any and every decision that you face. And finally, that's all you need to face the decisions in life.

> *"I keep coming back to integrity and the total combination of all my resources that make up my being"*

Prayer: "Center of life, permeate all that I am. Bring together in wisdom and compassion the decisions that I make. Grow my love and justice to become stronger options in this world. In the context of unity, keep trying."

Day 19

Psalm 40: 1 – 11 *"Sacrifice and offering you do not desire…I delight to do your will, O my God, your law is within my heart."*

The Psalmist knew that burning animals and giving money to the Temple were not what God wanted. Those things made no impact on the Divine. The Psalmist understood that what humans did with their lives would make a difference in the world. Thus he proclaimed that the presence of Divine will, which was already in the heart of the believer, is what would make a difference.

This reaffirms how important is the center—the heart, the pulling together of knowledge, experience, and will within a person. Again it is the recognition of a person's inner life as the source for whatever is done by that individual. Responsibility for one's actions cannot be blamed on someone else or some outside source. No matter how strong the external power and whatever the consequences may be, a person is still in charge of what they do. Thus God's peace, grace, and love are crucial in transforming one's inner life and attitude.

Prayer: "O inner source of my power, bring harmony within my spirit through the blending of will, hope, and wisdom. In the strength of a life focused on love and justice, go forth."

Day 20

Matthew 10:1-7 *"Proclaim the good news, the kingdom of heaven is at hand."*

This is one of the most inspiring passages in the whole Bible. But the sentence is also encrusted with obsolete interpretations that no longer speak to people. This sentence is commonly understood as the command to go into the world and preach a belief in Jesus as the Savior of the world. Followers are to promise that anyone who adopts this belief will be given eternal life in heaven as one of God's favored.

You don't have to act on the beliefs, for the requirement is only to affirm the statement as true. However, it's at this point that we need to go back to the early followers of Jesus and see what they meant with these terms and phrases. To begin, the first century peasants in Palestine were very familiar with the reign of Rome, or Babylon, or some other imperial power. Because they were on the route between these powers of the world, they were usually paying tribute to one or the other.

Many of the early followers had adopted the belief that only in heaven or an after-life would they have any kind of fulfillment. Their religious faith was to keep them loyal to a deity of life-after-death and prepare them for that time. When Jesus came talking about a rule that was already present, it shifted the focus in life from some future idealized state to their contemporary every-day world.

All they needed were the personal relationships--caring for one another, loving and being loved by the people around them, and finding meaning in the small events of their daily living. This understanding was 'Good News' and the command to share it with others around them became joyous as they simply talked about their new perspective on life and how that made them full of hope and love.

> *The newer paradigm is that a Divine experience simply uses the multiple resources within your body, mind, and spirit to pull together a new combination of understanding and will.*

Modern science and psychology have taught us to understand that the brain is where all the feelings, memories, and thoughts come together in every person. This is where values are held, judgments are made, and actions begin for every single individual. Thus it is also the location where that encounter with the Divine occurs.

It leaves responsibility with the individual for whatever actions or non-actions come forth. There can be great joy in living and sharing this understanding because it is 'good news' about what's most important in life and most fulfilling in the reign of the Divine!

Prayer: "Peace beyond the sense of knowing and feeling, fill me with the assurance that my life is important for just what it is and that I am loved in a way that brings meaning to who I am. In the knowledge of all that is loving, affirm life."

Ephesians 3: 14 – 21 *"I pray that you…may know the love of Christ that surpasses knowledge so that you may be filled with all the fullness of God."*

Paul usually begins a faith statement like that above with a reference to the human Jesus, whom he inter-changeably names Christ or Jesus Christ. Then he uses an example out of human experience to move on to how that enhances our knowledge of the Divine.

> *Paul is describing what happens when you become fully aware that you already have the fullness of life within yourself.*

Here the reference is to loving or being loved by Christ in such a way that it is beyond our capability to describe. He concludes that this experience is readily available to anyone who actually feels the presence of the Divine in life.

For todays faithful, it is describing what happens when you become aware that the fullness of life is within your recognition. Receive that gift and it can change your whole attitude toward daily living.

Prayer: "Giver of all gifts, fill me with awe at what I am experiencing. Challenge me to understand this sense of fullness as the reality of every day life. In the beauty of this day, affirm it."

Day 22

Exodus 15: 20 – 21 *"Sing to the Lord, for he has triumphed gloriously."*

The act of singing and dancing is a pulling together of many feelings, memories, impulses, and muscles in order for a different sound or movement to come out of the body. Whatever a person produces with the sound, it has required determination. That person is risking himself or herself because it will sound different than regular talking in conversation.

In singing or dancing, whatever comes out is the person's attempt to express joy and thanksgiving for what has been happening in their life. It's an acknowledgement that the experience has been good and that the person wants to express their happiness.

Perhaps that's why singing is so important in worship; it summarizes a lot of different things going on in your life. It says, 'I'm thankful for these things in my life and I want to celebrate the internal combination of energies that have allowed this to happen.'

Prayer: "Creative force that resides within me, I have much for which I am thankful. Use these gifts in joy and demonstration to become a sign for any to see and emulate. In the greater presence of all that is loving, use my energy."

Psalm 43 *"O send out your light and your truth, Let them lead me."*

The poetry in the Psalms explores so many ways to think about the relationship between the Divine and we humans. For instance, 'What is being requested in this metaphor of 'wanting God's light and truth'?

> *Seeking the light and truth of the Divine is wanting to follow what is the better direction in a world desperate for justice and love.*

It strikes me that the image--'Light of the Divine'--is a plea for clarity when everything around seems confused and filled with uncertainty. The contrast, of course, is darkness where you cannot make out choices or defend yourself from any threats. Asking for 'the truth of God' is seeking to understand what is really happening in your world. Then an alignment can be made that places you in harmony with the greater needs of the world.

Seeking the light and truth of the Divine is wanting to follow what is the better direction for you in a world desperate for justice and love.

Prayer: "Unifier of who I am, grant me the will and ability to see what is really happening around me. Utilize my thinking and responding in love and hope. In the possibility of a full life, yes."

Day 24

Acts 20: 17 – 35 *"If only I may finish my course...to testify to the good news of God's grace."*

Paul's testimony was always to be a person of faith in whatever situation he found himself. The fact of joyous weeping whenever he left one location and moved on is evidence of his personal integrity. The people knew that his life had been a tremendous value to them while he was present. This witness had made a difference in their lives.

During Paul's time—45 to 60 CE, Christianity was still in its initial stages of development. There were many people trying to form what they thought was its essential nature. The intensity of Paul's argument was to support his position—your life must show a loving attitude toward all people.

For Paul, the key to who he was and what he had to offer was an understanding of how Divine grace worked in a person's life. It was the sense that everything was a gift from God and this took away any need to proclaim or boast on your own successes. Humility reveals itself in personality as confidence and outgoing love all the time. That attitude can be imitated. It has the power to change the world.

Prayer: "Center of all that is, strengthen me for the journey that only I can take. Push me into avenues of service that I overlook. In the love that springs forth from gratitude, be daring."

Day 25

Matthew 10: 24 – 33 *"Rather, fear him who can destroy both soul and body in hell."*

I suspect this is not authentic from Jesus because he didn't talk much about hell. But the sentiment that 'the soul', 'the spirit', or 'the center' of what pulls a person together is more important than what your body does sounds consistent with what Jesus taught his disciples.

The Oxford don, C.S. Lewis, wrote a humorous exposition called 'THE SCREWTAPE LETTERS' not long after he became a Christian in the 1940's. These were fictional letters from an old experienced devil to his nephew who was just learning to be a skillful devil. Lewis had the old fellow teaching how to take a normal human impulse like helping a neighbor and turn it into a selfish grab for power. That's 'Devil Training 101'.

It's that inner attitude and sense of values that make a person who they are. Any time that this inner core can be diverted or turned into selfishness is when you need to rethink and reaffirm basic values. Otherwise they become vulnerable to passing fancies and lose their anchor in the test with many alternatives.

Prayer: "Deepest spirit that sits beyond every level of consciousness, keep ever before me the reality of my totality so that I may find joy and fulfillment in the choices I make. In the confidence of your presence, go to it."

Day 26

Exodus 33: 12 – 17 *"If I have found favor in your sight, show me your ways so that I may know you and find favor in your sight."*

What happens when one is dialoguing with the Divine? Is it an actual exchange of thoughts? Is it conversation with another being? What is it?

During my whole life until recently, I had assumed that my spiritual life was dealing with an entity that was separate from me. I tried to be open to that entity, wanted to learn from the greater wisdom of that being, and hoped that I could follow whatever guidance was coming from the Divine.

Now that my understanding of the Divine has shifted from external to internal, it looks different as I encounter the Divine. It's no longer seeking something new from any outside source. The prospect of Divine making a human encounter is about how to look deeper and in more places within myself in order to arrive at a new conclusion to whatever is the issue. This brings a new confidence to me. It also challenges me on where I expect to receive new motivations…from within the self!

Prayer: "Creative presence that is behind everything, keep ever before me the knowledge that my life starts with all my past history. Unfold my future through the coming together of my past with current observations. In the sense of a fuller experience of life, expand my horizons."

Psalms 84: 1 – 12 *"The Lord God is a sun and shield; he bestows favor and honor."*

Here is an acknowledgement of the utter subjectivity of religious faith. Calling God a 'sun and shield' shows the perspective of the writer. He experiences the power and grace of an inner resource. He also feels the sun as protection of personal faith from whatever might attack and try to tear down his integrity.

This attitude calls for self-reliance that is built upon a lifetime of responsibility and boldness in facing the difficulties of ordinary living. The confidence that you develop over time is the protective shield that allows you to face new and unknown challenges with only personal resources at hand.

If your faith can provide a way in which you can deal with the unknowns of health, personal relationships, possibilities, and challenges, then you can live as a favored or privileged person. You have been honored and given a means to rejoice in life under any conditions that may be forthcoming.

Prayer: "Bringer of joy into life, affirm my journey through the difficulties and challenges that have brought me to this day. Through this presence allow me to rejoice in just who I am. In the assurance that love is the final purpose in life, so be it."

Day 28

Romans 10: 9 – 10 *"For there is no distinction between Jew and Greek; the same Lord is Lord of all and is generous to all who call on him."*

These days the distinction that jumps into mind from this passage is the one between Christians and Muslims. It is so easy to lump everyone of a different faith into one mold. Then you can categorize them in such a way that you control how to think about a mass of people who are actually diverse.

My struggle is with the terrorists who have done the same thing with anyone who is a Christian or from the West. The difficulty is in assumptions—a conviction that anyone who is Christian is wrong and therefore should die. Or assuming anyone who is Muslim is suspicious and likely my enemy.

This line from Paul has the condition that one must first seek the blessing of the Lord. Deep within this understanding is a concept of Divinity that should be examined. Paul's conviction is that the mysterious force within each of us loves every last person on the face of the earth. Thus the more we listen to that inner source, the more we become loving in our personality.

Prayer: "Center of all life, take me beyond thought and reasoning to the core of all that I am. Build bonds of love and caring for every other creature. In the hope and confidence that love creates more love, live it."

Day 29

Matthew 20: 25 – 28 *"…Whoever wishes to be great among you must be your servant."*

I don't think Jesus ever said these words. It sounds too much like a squabble that broke out among the Apostles after his death.

However, it's an important thought from the author because it deals with how pride and selfishness can break out in any situation requiring leadership. Pride and selfishness are natural in each of us as we evaluate what we've done and what we're worth or what we would like to love. This is where Jesus tried to turn over the time-observed practice of putting oneself first. The ideal practice in a 'Jesus community' was to serve and care for the others. What the others needed, not wanted, was the new criteria for Jesus' followers.

Unfortunately, the history of the Church has reflected this struggle right down through the present with its leadership. Perhaps the only correction is to never give absolute power to one person; it has to be shared.

Prayer: "Developing strength within my soul, keep me always vigilant against the temptation to build up my status at the expense of the needs of my community. In the confidence of love's better purpose, be alert."

Day 30

Numbers 11: 16 – 17, 24 – 25a *"Gather for me 70 of the elders of the people… and I will take some of the spirit and put it on them."*

Jews and Christians for a long time have experienced the need for working together in order to achieve maximum efforts and benefits. This scripture setting was Moses getting worn out, but the same thing is true for anyone thinking he or she is the only person capable of getting something done.

In fact, it's the small number of people who learn how to share leadership and encourage development in others that become the best role models. Giving another person their freedom with responsibility is the instigator of real change in the world.

This continues to be true in every situation where people find themselves together with others in some form of community. The 'Spirit of God' is given to anyone who opens up to new possibilities for the greater good of community.

Prayer: "Giver of new insight, pour out the marvel of cooperation with diversity. Keep revealing new possibilities through the different life experiences of a community built on trust. In the surprise and excitement of exploring unity, it works."

Day 31

Psalm 96: 1 – 13

"He is coming to judge the earth.
He will judge the world with righteousness,
and the peoples with his truth."

The second line repetition in Hebrew poetry restates and reinforces the writer's conviction that the Divine Creator is the authority over the earth. This judgment will be fair to all. It gives substance to the Jewish-Christian claim that there are consequences in the world over how people live their lives. These actions will come with equity upon everyone.

This is a hard lesson to learn, as in global warming. The misuse of fossil fuels and the subjugation of millions of people demonstrate over and over that humans have selfishly used the resources of our planet.

This very difficult lesson to embrace is that actions by a person, a tribe, or a nation bear consequences in global terms. Even the effects of just living demand a better understanding and co-operation from all of us.

Prayer: "Maker of the interconnectedness of life, keep on revealing in more vivid images the ways in which the world is put together. Open us to the human responsibility of caring for the whole earth. In the joy of greater good with the wonders of full living, enjoy it."

Day 32

Romans 12: 1 – 18 *"Do not be conformed by this world but be transformed by the renewing of your minds so that you may discern what is the will of God—what is good and acceptable and perfect."*

> *"We are created to be responsible*
> *for living full and productive lives*
> *out of who we are."*

Again, Paul is putting responsibility upon us. Then he shows how we can make judgments that are necessary to have a full and productive life as a person of faith. It's not some external force or mysterious power that is to guide our lives. Paul says the changing of our attitudes will produce different actions and directions. Our attitude demonstrates our level of commitment, wisdom, and dedication. By thinking through whatever issue we face and making the best decision we can with the skills and abilities we possess, then we are doing the will of the Divine.

God doesn't want robots to act out some preordained scenario, but we are created to be responsible for living full and productive lives out of who we are.

Prayer: "Holder of all my potential, open my thinking to the wider needs of the world. Bring together my response as part of a contribution toward building an environment of love and support. For the sake of those not yet imagined, be real."

Esther 4:10-17 *"Who knows? Perhaps you have come to royal dignity for just such a time as this."*

The epic of Esther appears to be summarized in this passage about life-purpose. It dramatically places the Queen in the difficult dilemma of either being obedient to her husband or being faithful to her native people, the Jews.

> *'What is the most important value—a human made decree, or the existence of a living people?'*

The dilemma is over conflicting loyalties and the dangerous consequences to her if she breaks the king's decree. Breaking the king's law could cost her the loss of her own life.

The prophetic phrase of Malachi above puts her choice in religious and theological terms. 'What is the most important value for you in this particular situation—a human made decree, or the existence of a living people?'

That's still a major issue in decisions faced by people all the time. Should we allow human-made decrees to rule absolutely or should we stand for larger values that protect life and the opportunities for human growth?

Prayer: "Giver of my substance, reveal to me the potential within and bring it together. May it be an example to those who have been bullied and denied their rightful opportunities? In the greater good that comes in your wholeness, use me.

John 20: 19 – 23 *"Receive the Holy Spirit."*

This phrase is one of the most important sayings in the gospel of John. The writer puts these words on the lips of Jesus during his first appearance to the whole group on the day of resurrection. It is a saying from the earliest Christian communities that was formative for a new Christian. To experience the Spirit of the Divine meant that one had opened himself or herself to a reality in life that changed the way everything was seen and understood. It meant they had access to the same possibilities in life as had Jesus. His style of loving was their model for how life should be lived. It was to happen during their everyday living.

> *"You already have everything you need"*

Our time has fixated on what Jesus looked like and the conflicts he had with the priests rather than the affirmations he gave in his encounters with all sorts of personalities.

We need to start again with an affirmation: you already have everything you need.

Prayer: "Completer of all my potentials, grant me a fresh look at each situation I encounter. Shower my life anew every day with the fullness that is around me. In the name of creative love, live it."

Day 35

Psalm 99: 1 – 9 *"You have established equity; you have executed justice and righteousness in Jacob…Holy is he!*

'Equity' is one of those words I use and just assume that I know what it means; yet I seldom pause to think about what it conveys. The dictionary makes a reference to 'natural law', which I take to mean 'that's the way things are'. Another way to understand equity is to remember that all things— animals or plants—received the same options in their environment.

"Justice' is another way to equity, as in Hebrew poetry where thoughts are expressed in couplets. Here the idea of justice seems a bit more into the realm of human activity, so the emphasis on righteousness is definitely referring to how people relate to other people.

The bottom line is that everyone and everything receives the same opportunity to live out their potential. That is what makes creation 'holy'.

Prayer: "Gracious power within, use the talents and strengths within me. Develop my potential to act lovingly toward the people around me. In the inter-relatedness of all things, so be it."

Day 36

I Timothy 4: 12b – 16 *"Do not neglect the gift that is in you."*

This letter was addressed to people who were new to the faith. It gives a lot of advice on how they are to act toward each other and what practices they should emphasize in order to grow in the faith. Yet at the same time there is this emphasis upon using 'the gift' that is already within each one of them. The writer wants them to rely on themselves for making decisions on how they are to act. Then he adds suggestions on what this should include.

The traditions and practices of the Christian community are the setting in which all persons of faith live their lives. There are examples from which one may learn. But also in that context is the assurance that every person has already been given a gift. They are to use that gift in making their own decisions. This is another statement telling them that they are on their own in pulling together their resources, making decisions, and acting with love.

Prayer: "Creative Source that is, take me on a journey that sees with the heart. Cause my responses to life to be filled with beauty, broader understanding, and compassion for what is around me. May that compassion grow until it extends beyond what I can see into the whole world, mold me."

Day 37

John 21: 15 – 19 *"Follow me"*.

The fourth gospel ends with this conversation between Jesus and Peter and it symbolizes the intent of his whole writing. By placing this event between Jesus and the most crucial disciple, the writer concludes with a simple admonition that summarizes all Jesus' teachings while he was present with his disciples—"MODEL YOUR LIFE ON ME."

It is an acknowledgment that Jesus was not about teaching new laws or establishing a new power system. His disciples were to remember how he lived, the way he gave assurance to those he encountered, and the way he could love each person. He was willing to extend himself whenever he saw a need. Then he would include them in the growing circle of his community.

It's a summary for today's followers also. We are to keep going back to the way he lived, how he opened himself to every encounter, and relied on his sense of what was needed as the way to a fulfilled life. Can we follow that way?

Prayer: "Wholeness within my being, lead me to trust my total life with what I have become. Cause the decisions I make to reflect love for the created world and all those who need my help. In the memory of Jesus, my model and guide, dare to live it."

Day 38

Isaiah 43: 8-13 "You are my witnesses, says the Lord."

The prophets uttered their sayings as if the Divine was standing directly in front of the listener. They would speak directly to the person or persons so that there could be no mistake as to whom the words were addressed.

> *Life still demands consistency in behavior if others are to hear what you say with words and believe them to be true.*

This passage is about testifying to the one and only god, Yahweh. In a world where every tribe had its own divinity, here is Israel claiming that there is only one divine source. This God is behind everything that has been and will be created—there are no others! That's an audacious claim! The prophet is saying that it is the whole people of Israel who are to embody this understanding in the way they live their lives.

Life still demands consistency in behavior if others are to hear what you say with words and believe them to be true. Actions do speak louder than words and any claim to wisdom must be borne by the lifestyle of the initiator.

Prayer: "Sense of relatedness to all, focus my thoughts and decisions. Empower what I do to show an understanding of your commitment to building a loving world. In the hope for unity and joy, stay focused."

Hebrews 12: 1 – 6, 12 – 14 *"Let us run with perseverance the race that is set before us, looking to Jesus the pioneer and perfecter of our faith…"*

The writer of this letter wanted to build hope and confidence in his readers that they could face the difficulties of their situations, whatever they might be. To 'run with perseverance' is a pat on the shoulder telling them that they can survive any obstacle that falls before them. The assurance that he offers them is to reflect on Jesus' life and his example of living through obstacles that he faced. From within himself, he found the strength necessary for any situation.

> *There is nothing you will face that can overcome the strength of a life based on personal integrity*

For our time, it is still a good reminder that we also have the example of a real person who faced his life, persecutions, and even death. Jesus' life is a victory over whatever was thrown against him. Remember, there is nothing you will face that can overcome the strength of a life based on personal integrity'."

Prayer: "Holder of spirit strength, make me bold in setting forth on the tasks of my life. Expend my energies in the infinite possibilities of wholeness, be brave."

Day 40

I Peter 4: 7 – 11 *"Like good stewards of the manifold grace of God, serve one another with whatever gift each of you has received."*

The writer is trying to encourage an early group of followers to work together as a community. The idea is that everyone makes a contribution for the good of the whole. As each person is different, they possess different levels of skills and leadership. Each is to contribute whatever they can. Out of an understanding that they have received many gifts from the Divine, each is to share their gift with the community for its benefit.

It still holds that each of us has received different gifts. It makes for a stronger community when each of us can contribute out of our abilities to the larger good of the whole.

What we know from other parts of the 'good news' is that 'community' is now extended to the whole world. So how can we share who we are with the whole world? It begins with loving others as ourselves.

Prayer: "Presence beyond all knowing, cause my actions to flow out of the resources I have. May my gifts be shared with the larger community for the sake of just offering them. In the wholeness that is life, be filled."

John 17: 1 – 9 *"This is eternal life, that they may know you, the only true God and Jesus Christ whom you have sent."*

Jesus talked about himself as the son of man or the human one, never as the Messiah. So this passage had to come from the author of the Fourth Gospel, not Jesus. It is therefore representative of the Johannine faith community of around 90 - 100 CE.

Its significance is in what it tells us about how the early Christian communities had begun to talk about Jesus. They still considered themselves followers of 'the way', but they had added to Jesus as the leader of 'the way' the understanding that Jesus also was the human person who showed them the Divine. God was no longer an abstract concept, but the Divine that could be experienced and known in a human being.

I think the implications for today are crucial because it shifts our search for the Divine away from a source somewhere 'out there'. The journey for each of us is to experience the fullness of life available every day.

Prayer: "Beloved center within my life, spring forth in the creativity of love. Reveal every opportunity as a new expression of caring and fullness toward life itself. In the potential wanting to be expressed, go for it."

Day 42

I Peter 5: 1 – 11 *"All of you must clothe yourselves with humility in your dealings with one another, for 'God opposes the proud, But gives grace to the humble.'"*

The writer here is trying to put some practical advice into theological language. It appears their community has been spending much of its time and energy squabbling over who is the most important. This sounds like what we would call a dysfunctional family that can't show any respect for one another.

Each of us can recognize when someone starts acting like they're better than every one else, but it's difficult to notice or control that in yourself. The writer is saying that this really comes from a deep level of insecurity and that what is more basic is the instinct to be just who you are. That's more 'natural' and the type of personality that the Divine honors with peace.

I think the message for today is to accept gratefully your own personality. Look for the gifts of others around you rather than barking orders. Together this builds a stronger community.

Prayer: "That which is always present, come forth in the honesty of meeting needs around me. Lead me to overcome pride and self-aggrandizement. In the name of love for my fellow journeymen, I can do it."

Day 43

Ezekiel 33: 1 – 9 *"You mortal, I have made a sentinel for the house of Israel; whenever you hear a word from my mouth, you shall give them warning from me."*

The key words in this passage are becoming a sentinel and warning the people when you perceive a message from the Divine. That's a tall responsibility for anyone to see himself or herself as the one responsible for perceiving any special messages from the Divine. Then to have the task of passing that on to the rest of your people is a double dread. It's going to cause you to stand apart from the crowd. Daring to tell that perception out loud to those around you, especially when it's not a pleasant word, is likely to bring an immediate negative response toward you personally.

That's the reason why there aren't many prophets around us these days or any in recent memory. The task is still the same: listen to your own instincts and intuitions; interpret those to yourself first; and then finally share them publicly through words and actions. Whew!

Prayer: "Mysterious power that is within my being, touch my strength and courage to come forth with the truths that change lives. In the assurance that your will calls each of us to wholeness, be bold."

John 13: 1 – 18 *"If I, your Lord and teacher, have washed your feet, you ought to wash one another's feet."*

The author of John likes to have Jesus demonstrate his teachings by examples. Washing someone's feet after a journey was the task of the lowliest slave because it was the dirtiest part of the body. Also, one was very careful not to touch another's body. Here is perhaps the most memorable of all his actions and no one who had his feet washed by Jesus would ever be the same again.

Thus the example of servanthood that Jesus advocated for his followers was clearly demonstrated in this symbolic act.

During the week when Pope Francis visited the United States, he demonstrated this principal when he spoke to the United Nations Council in the morning and then left a luncheon with the heads of states to go into New York City's lower end and serve lunch to 300 homeless people.

"Can the call to followers of Jesus be any clearer on what we are asked to exemplify?"

Prayer: "Truth-releaser that is deeply protected within my psyche. Release also the freedom that honesty nurtures in the spirit. Bring me one step nearer the wholeness that is intended in my creation. Spoken in the Name and power of forgiveness, as it is."

Day 45

John 12: 20 – 26 *"Very truly, I tell you, unless a grain of wheat falls into the earth and dies, it remains just a single grain; but if it dies it bears much fruit."*

This is another story out of the community's early memory of who Jesus was. It showed how he encouraged people to gain a fuller life by setting aside their own ambitions and serving the people around them. This was completely opposite to the world around these first century peasants who had to scratch out a meager subsistence to live.

The normal and natural human model was to acquire all you can, save it for only your family, and keep any surplus for possible future needs. Here the new tradition is to share everything with whoever is around you and that will produce untold abundance for those in your community.

This passage is still difficult to embody because it's contrary to every urge to build up our own resources. Our challenge is to learn that there's really enough for everyone's needs. The challenge is to find ways to implement this.

Prayer: "Spirit of Wonderment, continue to pull together different aspects of my experiences into new conclusions. Explode new opportunities for living so that every day is a joy to behold. In the name of Jesus the explorer, affirmative."

Day 46

John 20: 1 – 18 *"Mary! She turned to him and said 'Teacher!'"*

Perhaps this is the most personal encounter in the whole New Testament. The first word to Mary is only her name, but it is strongly phrased and cuts through her bewilderment as she recognizes the familiar voice of Jesus. Her response reveals the relationship and long-established bond between the two, as her only word is 'teacher'. That carries with it the love and admiration with which she held Jesus. One can imagine her response, as the explanation following tells why she should not hold on to him so tightly.

For our time, the importance of this passage is not what happened physically, but the recognition or opening of Mary's spirit to the presence of the Mentor in her life. Maybe it's a once-in-a-lifetime event, but I think it can occur many times. It happens whenever we're willing to open ourselves to having Jesus enter our lives as teacher and model.

Prayer: "Precious memory of my experiences, bring together all those strands and events that compose my being. May I consciously affirm the decision to hold Jesus as my life-model. With the combining of new opportunities, make history!"

The end, Thank you for the journey.

Scripture Table

SCRIPTURE	DAY	SCRIPTURE	DAY
ACTS 1: 21 - 26	6	JOHN 17: 1 - 9	41
ACTS 6: 2 - 7	16	JOHN 20: 1-18	46
ACTS 20: 17 - 35	24	JOHN 20: 19 - 23	34
COLOSSIANS 2: 6 - 9	7	JOHN 21: 15 - 19	37
EPHESIANS 2: 8 - 10	1	LUKE 11: 1 - 10	4
EPHESIANS 3: 14 - 21	21	LUKE 19: 45 - 47	15
ESTHER 4: 10 - 17	33	MATTHEW 9: 25 - 38	17
EXODUS 3: 1 - 18	18	MATTHEW 10: 1 - 7	20
EXODUS 15: 20 -21	22	MATTHEW 10: 24 - 33	25
EXODUS 33: 12 - 17	26	MATTHEW 20: 25 - 28	29
EZEKIEL 33: 1 - 9	43	NUMBERS 11: 16-17, 24-25a	30
HEBREWS 12: 1 - 6, 12 -14	39	PHILIPPIANS 2: 1 - 5	11
I CORINTHIANS 3: 10 - 17	12	PSALM 100	3
I PETER 4: 7 - 11	40	PSALM 25: 1 - 6	9
I PETER 5: 1 - 11	42	PSALM 40: 1 - 11	19
I TIMOTHY 4: 12B - 16	36	PSALM 43	23
ISAIAH 43: 8 - 13	38	PSALM 84: 1 - 12	27
ISAIAH 58: 1 - 11	14	PSALM 96: 1 - 13	31
JOHN 8: 31 - 38	2	PSALM 99: 1 - 9	35
JOHN 10: 1 - 10	5	ROMANS 8: 26 - 28	8
JOHN 12: 20 - 26	45	ROMANS 8: 31 - 34	10
JOHN 13: 1 - 18	44	ROMANS 10: 9 - 10	28
JOHN 14: 23 - 26	13	ROMANS 12: 1 - 18	32

About the Author

Lon Chesnutt spent his career as a United Methodist minister. He started first as a campus chaplain in Atlanta, GA; and then pastored churches in the Baltimore/Washington area for thirty years. Since retirement, his involvement in ministry has continued through teaching, projects, and social groups advocating diversity, personal involvement, and justice. He and his  wife, Evelyn, live in Charlestown Retirement Community, Catonsville, Maryland.

COMMENTS: The author would appreciate your reaction to these daily devotions. Please send them to me by email at 'lonchesnutt@yahoo.com'.

August, 2016

Printed in the United States
By Bookmasters